Acknowle(

I must first thank the Lord Jesus Christ for all that He has done in my life. Truly, without Him I can do nothing. Secondly, I want to thank my wife Becca and my family who have wonderfully supported and encouraged me in each and every spiritual endeavor I have ever undertaken. Thirdly, I want to thank my mom and dad who have been used by God to point me in the direction of the Lord all my life. Finally, I greatly appreciate all the folks who took time out of their own busy schedules to make this book possible, including Bro. Kurt Kennedy, Bro. Charlie Tinsley and Mrs. Cara Gates in particular. I am deeply in debt to each of you, and I am praying that our combined efforts will be blessing to God's people.

Table of Contents

Foreword   3
Introduction   5

PART I: The Mistake That Was Made
Ch. 1 The Anticipation   10
Ch. 2 The Situation   15
Ch. 3 The Application   20

PART II: The Mandate to Multiply
Ch. 4 Increase Is Expected   27
Ch. 5 Ingenuity Is Encouraged   32
Ch. 6 Importunity Is Essential   38

PART III: The Methods Still Matter
Ch. 7 An Explanation   44
Ch. 8 An Example: Methods Matter in Walking with God   48
Ch. 9 Another Example: Methods Matter concerning the   53
           Will of God
Ch. 10 A Final Example: Methods Matter when doing the 60
           Work of God

PART IV: The Meaning of the Message
Ch. 11 My Summary   65
Ch. 12 My Sadness   69

PART V: The Mentions Will Be Minimal
Ch. 13 Cannot Negotiate on Inspiration - *King James Bible* 73
Ch. 14 Cannot Negotiate Presentation - *Church Atmosphere* 76
Ch. 15 Cannot Negotiate our Affiliation - *Baptist*   78
Ch. 16 Cannot Negotiate about Separation - *Standards*   81
Ch. 17 Cannot Negotiate concerning Glorification - *Music*   83

Foreword
Dr. David Gibbs, Jr

DR. DAVID C. GIBBS, JR.
CLA Founder & President

I want to encourage you that we serve a God that has given us a book with the absolutes of God-The Bible, The Word of God that will not change for all eternity. Now, we are living in a culture that says everything is negotiable. Things in the Word of God are being questioned like never before. In this book, "Non-Negotiable", Tony Shirley is taking a stand, and it is time for each of us to take a stand on *"Thus saith the Lord."* What God has demanded we dare not change. It doesn't matter which way the culture goes we are not to be absorbed by this culture. Our job is not for the culture to reach us, but for us to reach this culture. The God of the impossible, the God with whom His

Word never changes has given us the truth. We have the absolutes, now it's time to stand for them!

Introduction

Catawba Falls

It was March of 2017 and a group of friends, seniors in high school nearing graduation, decided to take one of their last days together and spend it hiking up Catawba Falls in the Western North Carolina mountains. Before Dawson left the house, his mother repeatedly said, *"Be careful."* It was a beautiful day and they were having a wonderful time on the way up, talking, laughing, and making memories which were being documented almost moment by moment with the many selfies and picture poses. They finally reached the falls that they were looking for, and after some time, one of the young men told how that in the past he had climbed just a bit farther and had found an amazing spot that would allow you to actually stand behind the falling water. It was said to be a breathtaking experience, and in just a matter of minutes, Dawson forgot his mother's words and even ignored a warning sign that was in the path and decided, along with his friends, to make the "extra" climb. Once they safely made it to the climactic spot, the other guys agreed that he was telling the truth. It was truly an awesome sight. After some time and some pictures, the crew decided to head back down. Now, having made the journey this far with no real problems, one young man tells how that he wasn't being nearly as careful on the way out. Roots and small trees that he had held on to on the way up weren't being grabbed now. Instead of carefully bending his legs and watching his balance as he had on the way up, he was now quite nonchalantly standing straight up as he walked out. It was at this point that things took a drastic  turn…with one simple slip, Dawson began to fall. The others watched in horror as he fell about 10 feet to the next ledge where he hit his head, but rather than landing and stopping, his body just bounced and rolled farther down the falls. When it was all said and done, Dawson lay 30 feet below his friends, unconscious and waiting for medical personnel to get him off the mountain and to the hospital!

My purpose in writing this book is to simply offer the same

exhortation that Dawson's mom offered to him – *"Be careful!!!"* As I look around in these last days, I see more and more who are allowing their zeal for growth and expanded influence to cause them to let go of some of the rooted and grounded things that have served as a solid foundation for many years, and many are slipping.

I have broken the book into five distinct parts, starting with a little Christian fiction based on a story found in **II Kings 4** that I believe illustrates what is happening to many of us. Part two of the book explains that I fully understand that we are encouraged and exhorted by the word of God to continually strive to reach more, do more, and help more for the glory of God; however, in the third and fourth sections, I hope to show my heart in this area of making sure that in our zeal we remember that

<u>Some Things Must Be Non-Negotiable</u>.

Finally, in the last part of the book, just to give the reader a clear idea of what I am talking about, I give you my top five non-negotiable things. I pray you will be blessed by both the intent and content of this book.

Part I: THE MISTAKE THAT WAS MADE

Chapter 1: The Anticipation

Elisha & the Sons of the Prophets

II Kings 4:38-40 *"And Elisha came again to Gilgal: and there was a dearth in the land; and the sons of the prophets were sitting before him: and he said unto his servant, Set on the great pot, and seethe pottage for the sons of the prophets. And one went out into the field to gather herbs, and found a wild vine, and gathered thereof wild gourds his lap full, and came and shred them into the pot of pottage: for they knew them not. So they poured out for the men to eat. And it came to pass, as they were eating of the pottage, that they cried out, and said, O thou man of God, there is death in the pot. And they could not eat thereof."*

Imagine with me for a few minutes…

Berel has waited for this moment for years! Ever since he felt the Lord dealing with his heart as a young man sitting at the feet of his father listening to stories about the miraculous things God did through great, Jewish heroes like Moses and Elijah. From Moses at the Red Sea to his time spent alone with God on the mountain, from getting to see a glimpse of God's glory to his face shining from the experience, stories like Elijah praying and stopping the rain for three years to the legendary tale of the fire falling from Heaven and the great victory over the prophets of Baal on Mt. Carmel – all of this birthed something in his heart that just never seemed to go away.

It seemed at first like just the piqued interest of a boy's excited imagination, but through the years, God had reaffirmed to him over and over that it was much more than that – God wanted him to be a prophet! Now, here he is, not only a part of the school at Gilgal, not only bearing the great honor of being one of the *"sons of the prophets,"* but today ELISHA is coming! ELISHA!!!

The one who walked with Elijah and watched him be swept up into heaven by a chariot of fire! The one who parted the Jordan River with his master's mantle! The one who he just heard raised a young boy from the dead in a place called Shunem!!! Berel will get to sit at the feet of one of the wisest, most powerful, most amazing prophets in the history of the nation of Israel.

Thinking Points

1. Do you remember when God first began speaking to you about your call?

2. Are there some heroes of the faith that God used to inspire you like Moses and Elijah did for Berel?

3. Aren't you thankful for those faithful servants at whose feet you have been able to sit and learn?

Chapter 2: The Situation

"...found a wild vine, and gathered thereof wild gourds..."

After several hours of Elisha's captivating teaching, they break for lunch. It is at this point that things get interesting. Per the prophet's instructions, his servant begins to recruit the help of some of the students for the purpose of feeding the group, and Berel is one of the young men chosen for the task. He can hardly contain his excitement as he works shoulder to shoulder with Gehazi in trying to serve the prophet. Soon, however, Berel and his friends realize that there is not enough pottage to feed the entire group.

He says to the young man, *"What are we going to do? Elisha and Gehazi have chosen us to serve and feed the group. We must not fail."* They head out into the field to try and find some herbs with which they might fill the pot and meet the need. After some time, and having found nothing suitable yet, the young prophets were growing a little desperate. At just that moment, Berel stumbles upon a small patch of vines covered with strange gourds. It was similar to some they had used before, but was actually a variety that neither had ever seen. After a brief inspection, his friend asks, *"Do you think we could use these?"* Berel, feeling the pressure to produce, replies, *"Do we really have a choice? Hey, what if we mix it with what we already have?"* Just like that, a desperate decision was made.

As the young prophets passed through the line and began to eat, Berel and the others were thrilled to have had an opportunity to serve. The young prophets thanked them for the meal, and there was an initial sense of satisfaction as all the hungry were able to eat. Berel was so excited about what had happened that he had even begun to think that God Himself had led him to those gourds. Just when Elisha and Gehazi were about to take their part, the worst happened! One by one the young men clutched their stomachs and cried out in pain. Each one who had already started eating began to get sick. It soon became

thou man of God, O there is death in the pot

very obvious that this new thing that seemed to have saved them in their moment of crisis was, to their great horror, actually bringing death to the camp!

Thinking Points

1. Do you think Berel had pure motives?

2. Have you ever felt internal pressure to succeed or please someone to the point that it brought you near desperation?

3. Can you think of any idea you have tried in the past that initially seemed to be a good one only to prove later to have been a mistake?

Chapter 3: The Application

"What could go wrong?"

Thankfully we know from the Word of God that Elisha was able to miraculously heal the poisoned pottage and all was well. However, I want to emphasize the mistake made by Berel and his young friend. They were not trying to be rebellious. They did not know those gourds were poisonous and chose to use them anyway. No, absolutely not!!! They allowed their desire to please their master to drive them into desperation when they found something lacking. This desperation caused them to be willing to try some 'new thing' BEFORE they checked it out to see if it was safe. That was their mistake.

This happens to us in life all the time if we are not careful. Many years ago, before we had any money or any children (we still don't really have any money because now we have a pile of children!!!) we were asked by some friends to house-sit for them while they were on vacation. Along with enjoying the amenities of their magnificent home, we wanted to be sure and make our presence a blessing to them as well.

So, I went outside to mow the yard (mowed over a yellow jackets' nest and that got really exciting too, but that is a story for another day), and my wife set out to do some cleaning on the inside of the house. Shortly thereafter, she decided to run the dishwasher, which, growing up in financially challenged families neither of us had ever used before. As she searched the cabinets, she found out that there was no dishwasher detergent. There was something lacking that was preventing her from being a blessing to our friends. So, this desperation provoked her to try and solve the problem. In her zeal, she noticed regular dish detergent sitting on the sink and decided that would be an appropriate solution. *"What could go wrong?"* she thought. *"Soap is soap, right?"* The truth is that after starting the machine, it seemed that this had worked. The washing machine was running, the dishes were getting cleaned, and all SEEMED well. Sometime later, Becca left the living room where we were relaxing to step into the kitchen for something, and the noise that echoed from the other room struck fear into my heart. I'm not sure I had ever heard my name shouted with such intensity. I jumped from the chair and sprinted around the corner only to find my wife about knee deep in soap suds that had just about covered the entire kitchen! Needless to say, as we cleaned and cleaned and cleaned, we had learned a valuable lesson. Don't let a good desire and a perceived lack mixed with desperation cause you to be willing to just try anything in order to fix it. What a mistake.

The sad truth is that this same mistake is being made by many in the ministry today. They sit in their offices on Monday and go over in their minds what they perceived as a lacking from the day before. They fret over a lack of faces. *"Why is the crowd just not what it used to be?"* *"Why are we not growing like the church down the street?"* Some are stressed by their lack of funds. *"Why is the offering so low?"* *"How are we going to pay for the revival that is coming up?"* Furthermore, others continually fight the mental and spiritual battle over a lack of fruit. *"Why didn't anyone come to the altar?" "How come we haven't had anyone saved for a while?"* These are all legitimate concerns to those of us in ministry, but the problem is that, when they persist, they sometimes push the servants of the Lord into desperation mode. Our sincere desire to try and please the Lord and reach people with the Gospel motivates us to begin to search for the solution to our perceived problem. Let me reiterate, just like in our story, there is nothing wrong with this desire or this effort, but many find themselves just where Berel did... desperate enough to try

"Darkness and light can never be brought together to talk. Some things are not negotiable."
A.W. Tozer

any new thing BEFORE checking it out to make sure that it is safe. I am not, as you will see in the next part of the book, against trying new things. Unfortunately, though, many of these things seem to bring an initial sense of satisfaction – maybe the crowd does initially grow, maybe the offerings do initially increase – but when perpetuated, they many times bring destruction instead of production!!!

A. W. Tozer once said, *"The blessing of God is promised to the peacemaker, but the religious negotiator had better watch his step. Darkness and light can never be brought together to talk. Some things are not negotiable."* That is the purpose of this book. I want to simply offer a cry for carefulness.

Thinking Points

1. Do you see a lack somewhere in your life that keeps you constantly frustrated and sometimes discouraged?

2. Can you see how this could happen in the heart of anyone that was simply motivated to do a good job?

3. Is there anything in your mind right now that you would NOT even consider sacrificing for the sake of growth?

Part II: THE MANDATE TO MULTIPLY
Chapter 4: Increase Is Expected

Mark 11:13 "...seeing a fig tree afar off..."

As we study the Word of God, we see very clearly that God wants us to continually strive to reach all that we can with the good news of the Gospel. In **Matthew 25:14-27**, there is the parable of the talents. Most of you are familiar with the lesson, as the *"lord of the servants"* gave to each some talents. As the story progresses, the lord takes *"a journey"* and is gone for a while. During his absence, the first two servants take the talents and *"traded with them"* in such a way that they experienced some increase. As a matter of fact, both doubled what the master had given them. The last servant chose to simply hold on to what he had in hopes of being able to simply present it back to his master. I believe he hoped to be commended for not suffering any loss. When the lord returned, he commended the first two for being

"good and faithful" servants, but when presented by the last servant with the same talent he had given him to start with, the lord says, *"Thou wicked and slothful*

*servant ...Thou **OUGHTEST** therefore to have put my money to the exchangers, and then at my coming I should have received mine own **with usury**."* This shows us very clearly that OUR Lord expects some increase. In **Mark 11**, the Lord Jesus Christ curses a fig tree because when He noticed from afar that it already had leaves, He EXPECTED that there would be fruit on it. The Bible says, *"...he came, if haply he might find any thing thereon..."* Because the fig tree has fruit before it has leaves, the Lord knew that He and the Father had given this tree everything it needed to bring forth fruit (sunlight, rain, time, etc...), so he expected some increase. When no increase was found – **Matthew 21:19** says, *"...He found nothing thereon..."* – the Lord cut off the blessings!!! The next day the disciples saw it *"withered away."* I believe the Lord has the right to look at our lives, considering how blessed we are, and expect some increase.

Just like Berel in our original story, we should each have a desire to please our Master, and that ought to motivate us to want to experience increase.

Thinking Points

1. It should be the goal of every leader to help those under their influence hear the words "well done" at the Judgment Seat of Christ…is it yours?

2. Are there any "blessings" that God has poured out on you or your ministry that you are not allowing to produce any fruit?

3. Hasn't God given us everything we need to be fruitful?

Chapter 5: Ingenuity Is Encouraged

Early Plan → *Expanded Plan* → *Eventual Plan*

Ingenuity is often associated with the business world and for good reason. Companies pay a high price to innovate and find the next "BIG" thing or the next "NEW" process in an attempt to be more efficient in their perspective market. However, this idea of ingenuity is not a new one. In **Luke 14**, the Lord shows an example of ingenuity as he teaches another lesson to His followers about the *"kingdom of God."* This lesson uses an illustration about a *"certain man"* who *"made a great supper and bade many."* This man is excited for the event and desires to bring a large crowd to his house so that he might be a blessing to them. He wants the house filled! He plans to provide a lavish feast for all who will come, and as has been their cultural custom, they send out specific invitations to those close to them. When the day has arrived and the meal was prepared, he *"sent his servant…to say to them that were bidden, come; for all things are now ready."* If you are familiar with the story, then you know that this plan simply didn't work. Many of the invited people began to make excuses, and as a result, the house wasn't full. At this point, the "lord" of the story abandoned the cultural, original plan and instituted an expanded plan to try and fill the house. He commanded the servant, *"...Go out quickly into the streets and lanes of the city, and bring in hither the poor, and the maimed, and the halt, and the blind."* Once this was done, the servant hurried back with an update but, sadly had to report, *"...yet there is room."* Still discouraged by the lack of people, the father makes yet another adjustment to how they've always done it and proclaimed, *"...Go out into the highways and hedges, and compel them to come in, that my house may be filled."* He had changed his way of inviting, the crowd invited, and the scope of his invitation in an effort to fill the house.

I believe now that we understand we should be striving to be more, do more, and reach more for the Glory of God (increase is expected), we need to also realize that we may have to consider trying new or different things from time to time in order to meet this expectation. (*Those of you who are nervous right now just stay with me – I am not talking about compromising – When we get to the last part of the book, you will see where I am going with this.*) There was a time when taking an old school bus and picking up kids and bringing them to church was a "new thing." The hundreds of thousands who have been saved through the bus ministry are glad our fathers embraced that ingenuity. There was a time that simply using a microphone was a "new thing," but I'm glad our fathers were willing to make the adjustment. There was a time that preaching on the radio was a "new thing," but I'm thankful this method of ministry was employed and now we preach through all kinds of media to literally almost every part of the world. Now, I'm sure you understand that when

 we try a new thing, there is a learning curve and there can be hiccups along the way. Like the time the massive monitor (actually a large smart TV) mounted on the face of our balcony tapped into someone's

Netflix account and started showing something that I was afraid was about to be very inappropriate right in the middle of my message!!! These bumps in the road are not always sure tell signs that we need to throw in the towel, but rather chances to step back and reevaluate. You might think, *"I'd tear that thing off the wall and get that devil box out of God's house,"* but we simply investigated the situation, figured out what caused the problem, and used the screen again in the following services in a way that has been a blessing to all in attendance. We are living in a digitally saturated, visually stimulated society, and we need to find ways to take advantage of that in the work of the Lord. In this generation, one statistic says that *65% of people are visual learners*, and this can be used to our good if we will be willing to embrace some ingenuity. Whether in the realm of technology, security, outreach, etc…, we need to be willing to consider new ways to try and fill the house.

Thinking Points

1. Did the father "compromise" by simply expanding the outreach for the wedding feast?

2. Have there been new ideas that you never even considered using because it simply wasn't how it's been done?

3. Have you adapted to this digital age in any way in the last few years?

Chapter 6: Importunity Is Essential

Coach Tom Landry

Hall of Fame coach Tom Landry once said, *"A champion is simply someone who did not give up when they wanted to."* Having coached the Dallas Cowboys for 29 years, including 20 straight winning seasons, winning a total of 270 games which is tied for 3rd on the all-time wins list, and winning two Super Bowls, Coach Landry knows a thing or two about perseverance. As we strive to achieve these same levels of achievement in the work of the Lord (not for personal glory or to win some *"corruptible crown"* but for the glory of God and the good of others), we are going to have to understand the importance of importunity. In **Luke 11**, we learn that this word simply means a refusal to quit. It's a Bible word for perseverance which means you just *"keep on keepin on!!!"* What we need to understand is that no matter how creative our plan or program, and no matter how aggressive and passionate our efforts, according to **I Corinthians 3**, it is *"God that giveth the increase."*

The truth is, just like when the Children of Israel were told to follow the cloud, there will be times that God allows our progress to stall. There were days, according to **Numbers 10:12,** on which *"the cloud rested."* These were times that the will of God was for them to not experience any forward progress!!! Now, we know that God always has a reason for such decisions and it is always for our good. For example, God held them in place at Mt. Sinai for at least 50 days while He was communing with Moses up on the mountain and giving him the commandments and the law. In these times, we must be willing to persevere – we have to keep on doing all the things we know are right to do whether we are seeing any 'real' progress or not. In staying with the football theme, Hall of Fame NFL running back Walter Payton understood this principle. In his illustrious 13-year career, he ran for 16,726 yards – that's almost exactly 9 ½ miles (that makes me tired just thinking about it!!!) The amazing thing is that his career average is 4.4 yards per carry. That means that he ran that entire 9 ½ miles while getting knocked down every 4 yards!!! Now, we know he had some long runs, but he also had a ton of times that he didn't seem to make any progress. As a matter of fact, there were many times that he actually lost some ground, but what he understood was that *"if I get up and keep coming at them, one of these times, I will break a long run,"* and he did. It was this mentality that ran him all the way to the halls of Canton.

In our introductory story, I appreciate and applaud Berel's desire, perseverance, and willingness to try new things in order to meet the need. We must be willing to be creative and try to use new ideas, new programs, new technology, etc... to try and reach more people than ever with the Gospel. We must also be willing to work hard and put effort on our excitement if we hope to see any fruit that remains. We must understand, however, that ultimately the increase comes from the Lord. If He decides to let us go through a spell where the cloud is resting ...if He decides we have to take a few handoffs and be tackled for a loss, we must be willing to get up and continue to be faithful in the things of the Lord trusting in the promise of **Galatians 6:9** which says, *"And let us not be weary in well doing: for in due season we SHALL reap, IF we faint not."*

With all of that being said...

Thinking Points

1. Do you look back and see areas where you failed to exhibit importunity? Places you failed to persevere?

2. Walter Payton was motivated by the hope that if he kept on plugging away, a big run would eventually present itself. What "hope" do you have that drives you to keep on?

3. If the world can press on when things get tough simply to win the praise of man or a corruptible crown or trophy, how much more should we press on in the eternal work of God?

Part III: THE METHODS STILL MATTER
Chapter 7: An Explanation

Rev. Charles Fuller

II Corinthians 2:11 *"Lest Satan should get an advantage of us: for we are not ignorant of his devices."*

Now that we understand that God expects increase and exhorts us to labor to *"fill the house,"* I feel it is important to point out what I consider one of Satan's snares for those trying hard to please the Lord. It is a very effective *"device"* that I am afraid, much like in the story of Berel, can be dangerous to those who sincerely want to please the Lord but find themselves facing what appears to be a lack. The trap is that, **as we get fixated on the mission and seek new, ingenuitive ways to experience an increase, we get <u>so desperate</u> that we willingly embrace any new method that comes our way.** Again, I am NOT against new things. In his devotional called <u>Revival Today</u>, John Goetsch tells the story of Charles Fuller. He writes, *"The Old Fashioned Revival Hour was a beacon of truth for America during the Great Depression, World War II, and up to the late 1960's. Many preachers were skeptical of using this new tool called 'radio.'*

*They would preach that since the devil is 'the prince of the power of the air' (**Ephesians 2:2**), using radio would open oneself to Satan's power. But God would soon silence the critics and use Charles Fuller's ingenuity to spread the Gospel across the nation and around the world. The program, however, was cancelled the same year as Fuller's death, and a much-needed lighthouse in the land of radio dimmed its light. Thankfully, many preachers have picked up the baton of Charles Fuller as they continue to spread the Gospel all around the world through the tool of radio and other modern forms of media today."* Some new ideas are most definitely sent from the Lord, BUT we must understand that methods do matter to God!!! Just because our motivation is pure does NOT justify any means that we use to achieve the goal.

Thinking Points

1. Satan uses this "device" to try and trap the hearts of those who sincerely want to reach more. What other "device" of Satan have you discovered as you have been serving the Lord?

2. Have you felt desperate enough to try "anything?"

3. Bro. Fuller serves as our example. He checked out the "new thing" (radio) and decided that, even though it was often used for evil, it could be a great weapon for the Gospel. Is there anything like that in our world today?

Chapter 8: An Example (*Methods Matter In Walking with God*)

II Samuel 6:1-3 The story of David bringing the ark back to Jerusalem.

The Ark on the Cart

The morning sun rises early, but not before Uzzah is already awake. He could not sleep much last night because, for the first time in years, the Ark of God is leaving his house. Having watched his father and older brother tend to the ark for years, Uzzah knows the awesome and privileged responsibility they have been afforded, and furthermore, he understands that blessings go wherever the ark goes. Understandably there is a measure of sadness in his heart. There are mixed emotions however, because the orders were sent down from the king that he would be granted the honor of driving the cart that would be hauling the Ark of God back to the city of David. As he laced on his sandals, Uzzah thought, *"I know its really best for the kingdom. We can finally, as a nation, get back to seeking the Lord's guidance. It's the right thing to do, and I am honored to get to be a part."*

The first part of the journey was even better than he imagined. The king himself is leading the worship as they walk before the ark singing and playing on harps and psalteries and timbrels. There were even cymbals adding to the crescendo of the high notes. Honestly, it sent chills up his spine, and once again, Uzzah rejoiced at the wonderful opportunity that God had granted him. Just as a new song was about to start, Uzzah noticed the oxen began to stumble. Fearing the worst, without even a second thought, afraid the holy Ark of God might be desecrated or damaged by falling from the cart, he reached out his hand to steady it…It would be his last act of service to the Lord.

Confused and disturbed, the king stood silently over the lifeless body of Uzzah. His thoughts were racing – *"How could this happen? Why would God take his life for protecting the ark? This just doesn't seem right. How can I now take it home to my city?"* In this moment of frustration, King David makes the hasty decision to halt the entire project and places the ark in the home and care of Obed-edom. As a result, for the next three months David missed out on the blessings of God!!!

How did things get so messed up? How did we go from worship to weeping? Wasn't the motivation right? Weren't the men right? The answer to both is yes, but the problem was that the method was not right! Methods still matter to God, and when we take a purely worldly method and mix it with a Godly motivation, it often brings destruction.

Thinking Points

1. Why was Uzzah killed?

2. Do you believe that Uzzah's motivation was right? Did he have his heart in the right place?

3. Was the "new way," even though it was a more convenient way, a better way?

Chapter 9: Another Example (*Methods Matter Concerning the Will of God*)

"I will make thy seed as the dust of the Earth"

All the way back in **Genesis 12**, God promised Abraham *"...I will make of thee a great nation..."* Just one chapter later, God doubles down on the promise by saying, *"And I will make thy seed as the dust of the earth: so that if a man can number the dust of the earth, then shall thy seed also be numbered."* I believe that we would all agree God made very clear that His perfect will for Abraham was to have a child.

Isn't it wonderful when you have that kind of clarity from the Lord? I must admit that I often find myself battling a measure of fear of whether I have used proper discernment when trying to make major decisions in the will of God. When we KNOW that we KNOW God's will, it gives a certain central focus that is quite freeing. What happens however, when you know for sure it is the will of God, like Abraham did, but it just does not seem to be happening? If we are not careful, it can create another situation of desperation, and like Berel, we may be willing to try just about anything to help bring this "perfect will of God" to pass. Satan and our own deceitful heart will tell us, *"As long as you're trying to fulfill His will, it will be OK."*

That is what Abraham and Sarah thought when they concocted the Ishmael plan. Can you hear their conversation? Sarah may have said, *"It's allowed in our culture, Abraham. There is nothing wrong with it, and then you would have a son. Maybe that's what God had in mind all along. We can't just sit here and wait until we are too old to have children. We have to do something. It's the will of God for you to have an heir."* No doubt with some reservations, Abraham concedes and as a result a son is born. Their motivation was right and pure – they were trying to do the will of God. The man was a good man, called in the book of James the *"Friend of God."* Yet, in **Genesis 17:18-19**, the conversation between him and God did not go so well. The Bible says, *"And Abraham said*

"O that Ishmael might live before

unto God, O that Ishmael might live before thee! And God said, Sarah thy wife shall bear thee a son indeed; and thou shalt call his name Isaac: and I will establish my covenant with him for an everlasting covenant, and with his seed after him." Even in a sincere effort to fulfill the clearly known will of God, methods mattered to the Lord!!!

Abraham's grandson, Jacob, found himself in a similar dilemma many years later. The Lord Himself had prophesied about Jacob and his older brother while they were still in the womb that *"...the elder shall serve the younger."* When it came time for their father to pass on the blessing of the elder brother, rather than sitting down as a family and discussing what God had plainly laid out as His will, Jacob's own mom crafted a deceitful method for making sure Jacob got the blessing. Their plan worked, but the family relationships were strained and Jacob was forced to flee for his life. If we fast forward twenty years and a good bit of maturing, we find Jacob wrestling all night with the Lord and declaring in

Genesis 32:26, *"...I will not let thee go, except thou bless me."* I remember reading that many years ago and thinking, *"What do you need a blessing for, Jacob? Didn't you already get it when you tricked your dad?"* I believe the answer to that question is that when you use the wrong methods to obtain even what might be the will of God for your life, it somehow does not satisfy!!! The methods matter!!!

Let me see if I can illustrate it. Picture, if you would, a young adult man and lady who have fallen in love. Both come from Godly homes, have Godly parents, and faithfully attend a good church. They have prayed, fasted, searched the scriptures and have even counseled with their pastor and parents. They have all come to the conclusion that it is the will of God for them to be married. Let's assume, for sake of the illustration, that they are right. Now, the only hang up is that her father wants them to wait until the young man has worked a steady job for at least six months (not a ridiculous suggestion I'd say). What if the young couple, in their excitement and in their assured position of the will of God, decides to ignore the father's request and run off and get married without his blessing? Well, the truth is that things may work out fine down the road, but I believe we all know that, at least for a while, the relationships and celebration of this new marriage is not going to be what it could have been had they honored this Godly father's wishes. The poor method will have caused it to not be as satisfying as the will of God should have been for them.

Thinking Points

1. Knowing the will of God is a good thing, but do you understand how Satan could even use this knowledge to cause us to stumble?

2. Do you believe that Abraham and Sarah had pure motives?

3. Can you think of another situation where someone had the motivation to please the Lord but were tricked by Satan into doing something wrong?

Chapter 10: A Final Example (*Methods Matter When Doing the Work of God*)

Moses smote the Rock

Mahatma Ghandi once said, *"If I want to deprive you of your watch, I shall certainly have to fight for it; if I want to buy your watch, I shall have to pay for it; and if I want a gift, I shall have to plead for it; and, according to the **means** I employ, the watch is stolen property, my own property, or a donation. Thus we see three different results from three different means. **Will you still say that the means do not matter?**"* Obviously, I do not support Ghandi's doctrine, but this is a very insightful quote.

Some want to point to the motivation or even the end result as a justification for whatever means they employed in their endeavor. If we were to use that logic in the historical account found in **Numbers 20**, then we would walk away impressed and amazed at Moses. The multitude stood before him in dire need of a miracle. They were once again without water and their families and flocks were stranded in the desert facing the possibility of a horrible death. As was often the case, they handled this trial poorly and began to murmur against the leadership and even longed to be back in Egypt! After talking to the Lord, Moses steps up in front of the congregation, angrily rebukes them for their bad spirit, and then takes that very familiar *"rod of God"* and smites the rock twice. Immediately and miraculously, the Bible says, *"...and the water came out abundantly, and the congregation drank, and their beasts also."* Through the actions of this Man of God, the people were saved! Applying the logic mentioned earlier to this situation, we would say:

1. Moses is a good man.

2. Moses had a good motivation because he was trying to help the people with their need.

3. Moses was blessed by God and a miracle was performed that saved the whole congregation.

Looking at these three things, it would be assumed that God must have been approving of whatever means Moses used in this situation. The problem with this logic is that in the very next verse after the miracle (**Numbers 20:12**), God rebukes Moses for his actions (smiting the rock instead of speaking to it like he was told) and punishes him by not allowing him to enter the Promised Land!

Even when we are doing the work of God for the purpose of helping other people, methods matter to God.

Thinking Points

1. Once again, can you see the "lacking" in their lives that ultimately led to Moses' mistake?

2. Does the blessing of God on a situation (even miraculous blessings) automatically mean that God is pleased with the person or the plan?

3. Does the end justify the means?

Part IV THE MEANING OF THE MESSAGE
Chapter 11: My Summary

As I near the end of these thoughts, let me just pour out my heart a little. Jeremiah, the old weeping prophet, proclaimed, *"Mine eye affecteth my heart..."* One commentary explained Jeremiah's statement this way, *"What I see, I feel. I see nothing but misery; and I feel, in consequence, nothing but pain."* What Jeremiah was seeing in his day was grieving his heart. Not to over dramatize anything, but that is how I feel about this topic. I am seeing so many preachers, most with a sincere desire to reach more, win more, and do more for God, become so desperate in this effort that they are making the mistake of Berel. They are implementing any and every idea that comes along in an effort to try and solve the problem of their PERCEIVED lack. As a pastor, I know that pressure...I know that desire...I have felt that urge. The sad part for me is seeing that in the last several years, EVERYTHING has become a part of the bargaining. They will change, add, or remove anything if it offers the hope of some growth or increase. I have watched friends make complete 180° turns on things they once proclaimed were fundamental and doctrinal truths. The burden of my heart is simply to offer a concerned cry. I am 100% for trying to learn and apply anything that will help us reach more with the Gospel in these last days, however,

THERE MUST BE A FEW THINGS THAT ARE NOT ON THE NEGOTIATING TABLE.

Some things simply cannot be considered for compromise, even IF someone promises a boost in attendance or influence. NFL Hall of Famer and maybe the greatest wide receiver to ever play the game, Jerry Rice once said, *"I think my secret is that*  *there's no shortcuts for hard work..."* I am afraid we are looking for shortcuts in the ministry that are leading many to consider compromising on some things that should never even be a part of the discussion.

Thinking Points

1. Are you driven to do more, reach more, and see more saved than ever before?

2. Have you seen any of your friends make drastic turns away from beliefs they once held?

3. Do you agree that there must be *SOME* things that are non-negotiable?

Chapter 12: My Sadness

If I may, I want to step out of my role as "author" for a few minutes and simply speak as a friend. It both saddens and scares me as I watch preachers and Christians fall into this snare of the devil. As I see them begin to negotiate on some things in the name of appeasing the desires of this new age or the sensitivities of this new age, I am burdened and afraid about where the line will eventually be drawn, if a line is ever drawn at all. If someone suggests something like changing the name on our church sign to be less offensive, and that it would probably bring more people into our congregation, I wonder how long it would be before someone else steps in and adds, *"If you'd just stop preaching on (you fill in the blank) then more people will probably come too."* I am not trying to be judgmental, but it breaks my heart to see some who have had many people invest much time and attention into their lives begin to negotiate and trade away some of the foundational truths that have been preserved and passed down to them. I long to see some stand up as Naboth did to Ahab and say, *"I will not give thee the inheritance of my fathers."*

As I have written repeatedly, I am not against finding some new ways: new technology, new means of propagating the Gospel, or new  ways of meeting the needs of God's people; however, I am increasingly saddened and scared at the direction of Christianity in these days, particularly those who are part of the younger generations.

Dawson, the young man who fell from the falls in the opening story of this book, was miraculously uninjured from his fall, but sadly, in the spiritual world, we are not always so lucky.

Thinking Points

1. Do you see any trends in modern Christianity that concern you?

2. Like Naboth, we have been passed down some things that others labored to preserve for us. Would you be willing to trade them away?

3. Do you care enough to be careful?

Part V: THE MENTIONS WILL BE MINIMAL

Chapter 13: Cannot Negotiate on Inspiration

In closing, I am sure that many of you are wondering what "things" I am talking about. Now, remember, your list may be different than mine, but at least care enough to HAVE a list! Surely there are some things that are non-negotiable. I will put a list of five of my non-negotiables out just to simply illustrate what types of things I am referring to. Here we go...

Non-Negotiable #1: The King James Bible

We are promised in **Psalms 12:7** that the Word of God would be *"preserved...for ever."* I firmly believe that God has kept this promise in the form of the King James Bible. I believe it to be the inerrant, infallible, inspired Word of God. Because of that belief, I cannot allow the use of other versions of the Bible to enter any conversation about how to try and appeal to this new generation. It simply IS NOT up for negotiation in our church. I cannot even take the route of simply turning a blind eye if some want to teach Sunday School from other versions, etc... I believe the KJB to be the perfectly-preserved Word of God, and it is a non-negotiable! President Abraham Lincoln once said, *"In regard for this great Book, I have this to say, it is the best gift God has given to man."* Let us never negotiate with this great gift!!!

Chapter 14: Cannot Negotiate Presentation

Non-Negotiable #2: Changing the church look and atmosphere into a nightclub type environment

The Lord Jesus seemed very serious in the Gospels that the temple remained a *"house of prayer."* I believe that there should be a reverence given to the Lord's house, and it should be looked at and respected differently than other gathering places. What takes place here (the worship of the Lord and the preaching of the Word of God) is very important and needs to be given more respect and attention than what is given to social or entertainment gatherings. If we "dumb down" the atmosphere, we will automatically tear down the authority. Furthermore, I believe that if we have a real hope of MAKING a difference in the lives of people, then what they experience at the house of God needs to BE different than what they experienced out in the world the night before.

Chapter 15: Cannot Negotiate our Affiliation

Non-Negotiable #3: Being a Baptist

I realize that Baptists, particularly Independent Fundamental Baptist, have done ourselves no favors in the public relations realm, and as a result, the testimony of the Baptist name has been damaged over the last few years. With that being said, I was never an Independent Fundamental Baptist because it was popular. I am a Baptist because I believe in the ***Baptist Distinctives*** *(Bible as sole authority, Autonomous local churches, Priesthood of the believer, Two ordinances, Individual soul liberty, Saved & baptized church membership, Two offices, & Separation of Church & state),* and that these beliefs are the closest thing one can find to the Biblical, New Testament Church. I am not going to remove that name, even if it is just from the public eye, simply because some Baptists have behaved foolishly. I remember men like John Weatherford who was jailed and persecuted for standing on his Baptist beliefs in colonial Virginia. I wonder what he would think about the modern, young man who says, *"I just worry that people might not like it, so I'll just take it off the* *sign."* There have been many Americans who have acted like a fool throughout our history, but I am not willing to change my national allegiance because of them, and I would say the same about our denomination.

Chapter 16: Cannot Negotiate about Separation

> *"Wherefore come out from among them, and be ye <u>separate</u>, saith the Lord, and touch not the unclean thing..."*

Non-Negotiable #4: Removal of preaching and teaching Biblical separation and standards

I realize that many of us who say we believe in standards and separation would have disagreements, even among ourselves, as to what those should be. I am not here to have that debate today. My concern at this point is that there is a move to *NEVER* preach or teach on any type of standards of behavior anymore. People have started to abuse the grace of God and say that it simply doesn't matter how we dress, how we talk, or what we do any more. They say that we are "old fashioned" if we still hold to any semblance of modesty and temperance. Some would suggest that our crowds would no doubt grow if we would simply remove these things from our messages and lessons, but I will have to say that this is off the table. It is a non-negotiable. We may draw our "lines" in some slightly different places, but we *MUST* still at least have *SOME* lines.

Chapter 17: Cannot Negotiate Concerning Glorification

Non-Negotiable #5: Changing our music to the carnal/ worldly music being pushed in many churches today

I **DO NOT** want to be in a church that is dry and dead, but I fully believe there is a "place" between the carnal/worldly music (complete with full praise bands, flashing lights, etc…) and lifeless music. I want good, conservative, Christian music sung **FROM THE HEART WITH SOME HEART!** If we have to bring in a so-

> *"We need to sing FROM THE HEART WITH SOME HEART!!!"*
> **Pastor Tony Shirley**

called Christian rock/pop/rap artist in order to have a bigger crowd, then we will simply not experience that type of crowd. For me, this choice is a non-negotiable.

The five that I have mentioned are certainly not an exhaustive list for me, and furthermore, no doubt some have already thought that you would remove one and replace it with another that you feel is more vital and important. There is a good chance that I would agree with you completely, but the purpose of my list is to simply stimulate thinking and talking on the subject. Let's ask God to give us wisdom as to what things are non-negotiable and once that list has been made, let's get busy and creative in doing all we can to reach this generation with the best news anyone has ever heard – the Gospel of Jesus Christ. As a matter of fact, at the conclusion of the book is an opportunity for you to create a list for yourself. As God nails these things down in your heart, it may serve you well to revisit it from time to time to make sure that you haven't drifted from them.

Many years ago, I adopted some life goals from a message I heard preached by Pastor Rick DeMichele of Meridian, Idaho. He said it was his goal to *"finish and finish clean."* He simply stated that he did not want to blow his testimony and bring a reproach on the name of the Lord this near the finish line. I took those goals and have added one based on the Apostle Paul's words in **Acts 20:28** and made them my own. *I want to finish, finish clean, and finish with joy!* My prayer is that all of you are able to do the same to the glory of God and for the good of those we can reach. Be careful my friends, and God bless.

Thinking Points

1. Are some things non-negotiable?

2. What do you think about my list?

3. What things would you remove and what would you replace it with?

My Non-Negotiables

1._____

2._____

3._____

4._____

5._____

I Corinthians 15:58

*"Therefore, my beloved brethren, be ye stedfast, **unmoveable**, always abounding in the work of the Lord, forasmuch as ye know that your labour is not in vain in the Lord."*

Bibliography

1. All scripture is from the KJV of the Bible

2. Sweeting, George. (1995). *Who Said That?.* Chicago Il: Moody Press

3. Karr, Douglas. *"2014 Statistics and Trends for Businesses on Social Media".* Martec.Zone. October 1, 2014. Cleveland OH. Content Marketing World

4. Pro Football Hall of Fame Editors. "Walter Paton's Stats". profootballhof.com. 2019. Canton, Oh

5. Goestch, John and Birt, Nathan. (2019) *Revival Today.* Lancaster CA: Striving Together Publication